Lake District

A photographic journey around England's Lakeland

Dave Coates

MYRIAD BOOKS

Bassenthwaite and around Keswick

A natural starting point for visitors to the Lake District is Bassenthwaite, which is at the heart of this glorious corner of England. Interestingly, Bassenthwaite is the only stretch of water in the region that is referred to as a "lake" – all the others are "waters", "meres" or "tarns". *Giant Landscapes – the Lake District* takes a photographic tour through the Lakes, beginning with the hills and dales that surround the town of Keswick, at the head of Bassenthwaite Lake and going on to visit the beautiful Newlands Valley and the mysterious stone circle at Castlerigg.

Skiddaw on a winter's afternoon
One of the great fells near Keswick is Skiddaw, which stands at over 3,000ft (915m) and dominates the surrounding countryside. Seen here on a winter's afternoon, the soft watery sunlight plays on the landscape as sheep forage in the foreground.

Dodd Fell sunrise
Bassenthwaite is only 70ft (21m) deep and is fringed with rich vegetation. Once the sun has risen from the south-east over the fell the appearance of the lake changes dramatically. The sky becomes suffused with gorgeous orange and yellow hues while the lake and the mist also take on the same colours. Gradually the day begins to warm up.

May blossom in Newlands Valley

To the west of Keswick is Newlands Valley, shown here in the spring. There are no lakes here, just a lovely valley surrounded by the high fells. Cattle graze in the fields, while the May blossom in its full glory adds to the beauty of the landscape. The fell of Hindscarth rises up in the distance to create a perfect backdrop to this scene.

Newlands Valley

This photograph was taken on a dull and cold windblown November day. For some time there had been total cloud cover. Then suddenly, as often happens in the Lakes, alternate cloud and sunshine swept repeatedly over the same patch of landscape. The photograph, which is so enhanced by the dramatic effect of sunlight, was well worth the wait.

Blencathra in snow

The dramatic skyline of Blencathra is shown to good effect with the morning light bringing out the very best in this snow-clad landscape. In the foreground is an old section, now largely unused, of the A66 which leads to the heart of the northern lakes.

Autumn mists in the valley

Before the sun has risen high enough to reach over the surrounding fells and into the bottom of Newlands Valley, the mists on this September day combine with an early frost to give a quiet but wonderfully peaceful feel to the scene.

Summer morning at Castlerigg

To the east of Keswick on a raised shoulder of land, but surrounded on all sides by the high fells of the northern lakes, lies the ancient stone circle of Castlerigg. Formed from volcanic Borrowdale rock which was swept through the region by Ice Age glaciers, and dating from about 2000BC, the circle consists of 38 standing stones, with 10 at the centre. On this early morning in July, the sun has cast a soft but glowing light on the stones which only seems to add to the air of mystery that surrounds the scene.

Castlerigg stone circle in storm light
In this photograph the stone circle can be seen in the full glory of its dramatic setting. Here, the distant storm clouds over the Helvellyn range contrast with the sunlight on the stones.

Single stone and Skiddaw
The enigmatic shapes of the individual stones of the Castlerigg stone circle can take on a "sculptural" quality, especially when the sun is low in the sky. This stone, set against Skiddaw in the late afternoon sun, is a good example.

Derwent Water and Borrowdale

The north-eastern shore of Derwent Water lies at the very edge of Keswick and is directly upstream of Bassenthwaite Lake. Located beneath the fells of Catbells and Skiddaw it is one of the larger of the Lake District's lakes and at its widest point is 1¹/₄ miles (2.8km) across. Our journey continues towards the high fells with a visit to the valley of Borrowdale. The unique landscape of Borrowdale was formed by glacial action which resulted in a steep moraine gorge and a flood plain overlooked by dramatic fell scenery on all sides.

Winter – Skiddaw from the head of the lake
This is a typical picture of Derwent Water in the winter. On a clear day the winter colours of the reeds in the foreground contrast with the blue of the sky. This photograph was taken from the duckboards which carry the footpath across the vulnerable marshlands at the head of the lake. In the foreground there are icy pools with frosted grasses and reeds; in the distance are the peaks of Skiddaw and Walla Crag (1,243ft/379m).

Spring – Manesty Woods and Walla Crag
This photograph is taken at the south-western corner of Derwent Water near Manesty. The flowering gorse and fresh leaves on the trees tell us that spring has arrived with all the promise of summer to come. A still day adds to the mood with the mirror-like reflection of a welcoming blue sky and soft white clouds. Blencathra and Walla Crag take on a bluish hue as they stand in shadow in the background.

Summer – Derwent Water and the Jaws of Borrowdale

This photograph was taken on a fine summer's morning overlooking Derwent Water from Falcon Crag. There are glorious views in every direction at this location. The dazzling sky and still lake contribute to a feeling of peace as we look across to the Jaws of Borrowdale on the left and the fells of High Spy and Maiden Head on the far side.

Ashness Bridge

Ashness Bridge, on an ancient packhorse route, is a popular location for visitors to Derwent Water. The classic views of the stream and the bridge, coupled with the distant view of Derwent Water and Skiddaw, demonstrate why it is one of the Lake District's most popular spots. On a cold March day, the cloud cover gives only short breaks of sunlight, but the ever-changing patterns of light are always captivating.

Autumn – Blencathra from Manesty

Seen from the fells above Manesty, shortly after sunrise, Derwent Water is shrouded in autumn mists that seem to flow across the lake and cling to the flanks of Skiddaw and Blencathra. The gorse bushes, some still flowering well into autumn, seem to enhance the autumn colour of the trees below.

Ferry tied up in evening light

As one of the larger lakes, Derwent Water enjoys a scheduled ferry service to various points around the lake from the boat landings at Keswick. The late afternoon light has enhanced the colours of this scene with the ferry tied up at the Keswick boat landings. Both Skiddaw behind and the reflections in the water seem to glow in the warmth of the light.

Light and shadows from Honister Pass

The road through Borrowdale eventually climbs out of the valley towards Buttermere via the infamous Honister Pass with its steep road and reputation for rapid changes in the weather. This view looks back down and across Borrowdale from near the top of the pass. It was taken on a day with sun highlighting parts of the landscape.

River Derwent towards Cockley Howe

The River Derwent, which feeds into Derwent Water, flows down the rocky moraine gorge of Borrowdale. There is an ever-changing scene with trees clinging to the banks as the fells rise upwards from the course of the river. In this picture, looking down river towards Cockley Howe, the steep sides of the valley create an impressive backdrop with the bracken reflected in the water.

Grange Bridge in Borrowdale

Situated snugly in the bottom of the Borrowdale Gorge is the lovely village of Grange. The narrow but beautiful old bridge that gives access to the village from the main valley road is seen here basking in the midday sun, with the rugged sunlit fells behind only serving to emphasise the gorge-like nature of the location.

Borrowdale standing stone

In this area you will come across a number of standing stones – including the famous Bowder stone – deposited by Ice Age glaciers. The standing stone at the head of the gorge, pictured here, may have arrived naturally – although it looks as though it has been placed here by human hand, rather like the famous Castlerigg stone circle.

Buttermere and Crummock Water

At the head of Borrowdale our journey follows the main road that makes its dramatic climb out of the valley via Honister Pass and down into the Buttermere valley. This valley is closely surrounded by some of the most famous of the lakeland fells, such as Fleetwith Pike, Haystacks, Red Pike and Robinson. On a still day the lake acts like a mirror and the way the light plays into the valley from between the fell tops creates spectacular lighting conditions, adding to the beauty of this place. Crummock Water is the next lake downstream from Buttermere; less well-known than its illustrious neighbours, it is a wonderful place to linger – and an ideal spot to get away from the crowds.

Buttermere and Crummock Water from the descent path
Fleetwith Pike is located at the southern end of Buttermere. The return path from its flanks leads the fell-walker back to Gatesgarth Farm and offers this wonderful view of Buttermere with Crummock Water in the distance.

Innominate Tarn and Pillar with heather
Innominate Tarn (so-called because it has no name) is seen here in the middle distance with Pillar as a backdrop. This was one of the favourite places of the late Alfred Wainwright, the author of the classic guides to walking in the Lakes. It certainly is an atmospheric spot – wander through the rocky hummocks and a different view opens up at every turn.

Dubbs Quarry
It is easy to forget that the Lake District had an industrial past but here, high on the flanks of Fleetwith Pike (2,126ft/648m), which overlooks Buttermere, are the remains of a slate quarry. With a wonderful feel for the environment, one of the old ruined buildings has been tastefully renovated and turned into a mountain refuge hut. The tension between this and the ruins to the left add a touch of poignancy to the scene.

Autumn – the char hut and Gatesgarth
As autumn advances, the grasses fade and the bracken turns a rich golden brown. Looking across the head of the lake towards Gatesgarth Farm and Honister Pass, the autumn colours and the old char hut are reflected in the almost still water. The hut is used as a place for fishermen to store their gear and gets its name from the char – a fish which is a close relative of the trout or salmon, but much smaller in size.

Spring – Haystacks and the lake
The gorse bushes coming into flower signal the regeneration of spring and also form a natural foreground to this picture. It was taken in the early stillness of a May morning looking across the head of the lake towards Haystacks. At 1,732ft (528m) this was one of Wainwright's favourite places – so much so that he arranged to have his ashes scattered on Haystacks, by the side of Innominate Tarn.

Rannerdale Knotts and the peninsula

The surface of Crummock Water had almost stilled when this photograph was taken at about noon on a lovely late September day. The little peninsula of land that reaches out into the lake leads across to the rocky hummocks of Rannerdale Knotts and Whiteless Pike in the centre background.

Buttermere reflections in early autumn

The sight of Buttermere on a fine morning is breathtaking. The reflections from the steep fellsides are so real that you feel that you could almost step into them. The light and shadows cast by the low sun as it rises between the peaks creates a sight that is truly magnificent. Buttermere was once voted the second most beautiful place in England. But for many people, it is their favourite beauty spot.

Loweswater Fell

Loweswater Fell is one of the quietest and least visited corners of the Lake District. This photograph was taken on an autumn day when light was at a premium and the landscape was an ever-changing pattern of colour and shadow. Everything seemed to come together here, with the variety of colours on the scree balanced by the sheep grazing peacefully below. The solitary tree seems to emphasise the feeling of wilderness.

The last light of autumn (above)

One can often walk the fells on a dull day in the hope that at some point the sun will poke through the clouds just long enough for you to take a picture. It was such a day one November when we were walking on the fells alongside Langthwaite Green near Crummock Water. With the leaves almost gone from the trees this photograph could easily be named "the last light of autumn".

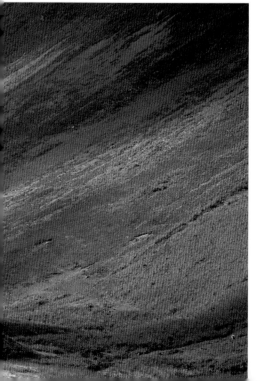

The thorn tree, looking toward Grasmoor and Whiteless Pike

The prevailing winds can bend exposed trees into some interesting shapes and this thorn tree on the fellside overlooking Crummock Water is a good example. The photograph was taken with the camera near to the ground so that it framed the view across the lake to the mass of Grasmoor. The little patch of cloud is a piece of good luck which helps complete the picture.

Wasdale, Eskdale and Duddon Valley

From the north-western lakes and valleys we now move south to explore the south-western valleys. We start with Wasdale, which has its own brand of dramatic scenery, reaching as it does to the foot of some of the high fells including Scafell, the highest mountain in England. We then move over the fells to Eskdale before crossing the Hardknott Pass to take a look at the Duddon Valley. Surrounded by wild fells, these two valleys do not contain any lakes but make up for this with their dramatic and breathtaking scenery.

Winter's light, Wastwater

As the nights shorten and the sun comes round into the south-west in the afternoon, Wastwater and its magnificent, if slightly forbidding, scree slopes can be seen at their very best. On a February afternoon with the wind blowing lazily but icily down the lake, the sun suddenly bursts from under an almost unbroken layer of cloud to provide this wonderfully lit view of Wastwater and its threatening slopes.

Duddon Valley Fells

On the left of the photograph is the shadowy form of Harter Fell. At 2,139ft (652m) it is one of the higher peaks of the central lakeland and dominates this view of Duddon Valley with the high fells of the Lake District in the distance. The rough, craggy and rock-strewn nature of Duddon Valley is clearly seen in this photograph taken from the road which leads over Kiln Bank and the Dunnerdale Fells.

Esk Falls, Eskdale

The Esk Falls, which carry the infant river on its journey down from Great Moss, are located just above Lincove Bridge. They are just one of a brace of sparkling waterfalls to be found at this location where the river passes through a narrow gorge.

The Upper Eskdale Valley

Park near the foot of Hardknott Pass and wander into the beautiful valley that is Upper Eskdale. The only sounds are of the wind and the water as it passes over numerous waterfalls. Although well-known as the starting point for hikers exploring the Scafell range, the less energetic can still enjoy the beauty of this peaceful dale surrounded by views of some of the grandest mountains of the Lake District.

Tarn Beck and the Seathwaite Fells

A popular walk in Duddon Valley takes you up the line of Tarn Beck and then onto the Seathwaite Fells. As you wander down from the parking area by the main road you come to a little footbridge which take you over the beck. Once onto the fells you find yourself in a geat bowl in the hills and ahead of you is the wall of fell that separates Duddon Valley from Coniston. The fell includes a number of well-known points of interest including the peaks of Swirl How (2,637ft/804m) and the Old Man of Coniston (2,364ft/803m). At your feet is Seathwaite Tarn. The tarn is about 800m in length and any surplus water is carried from it down Tarn Beck into Duddon valley.

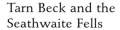

Coniston and Tarn Hows

From Duddon Valley we move over the range of fells dominated by the Old Man of Coniston to Coniston Water itself and to Tarn Hows, which lies nearby. The small town of Coniston – "king's village" – lies at the head of the lake and under the lea of the Old Man, whose lower slopes provided work for the town's inhabitants in its industrial past. The beautifully located waters of Tarn Hows were once actually three smaller tarns until, in the 19th century, their enterprising owner dammed the outflow and made them into the larger, but more splendid, single tarn that we see today.

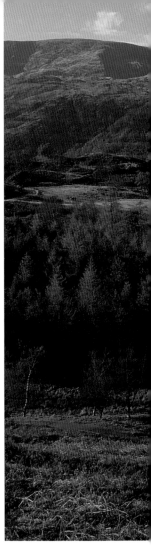

Coniston Town under the lea of the Old Man
Look more closely at those hills which seem to crowd over the homesteads of Coniston and you will realise that town and fell are deeply entwined in their industrial past. The waterfall that tumbles down the fell carrying Levers Water Beck towards the town flows past numerous old spoil heaps left over from times past when the copper mining industry held sway.

Coniston Water on a misty day
There are many days when the high peaks around Coniston seem to encourage a haze to settle over the narrow lake. And yet despite the mist, the natural beauty of the surroundings shines through and atmospheric images of the water and mountains appear in every direction.

Tarn Hows with Weatherlam

Tarn Hows, a collection of three tarns now merged into one, lies on the lower fells to the north of Coniston and must be one of the most visited of all the tarns in the Lakes. Beatrix Potter purchased the site as part of an estate and donated it to the National Trust. On this fine November morning, with the colours of autumn in the trees, the still water reflects the sky like a mirror. Weatherlam (2,500ft/762m) stands high in the background overlooking the tree-lined tarn.

Across the trees into Great Langdale

Great Langdale is one of the most spectacular valleys in the Lakes. This stunning landscape is a paradise for walkers and nature-lovers. Here the snow-dusted fells of Great Langdale seem to glow in the late afternoon light.

Tarn Hows shoreline

There are many beautiful scenes to be found on the shores of Tarn Hows. This little stand of silver birch trees in their autumn colours is vividly reflected in the still waters of the tarn and seems to stand out among the surrounding greenery.

17

The Langdales

T he Langdale Valleys lie just to the north of Tarn Hows and are in the very heart of the Lake District. The first valley, Little Langdale, is more popularly known for the narrow and tortuously winding route that takes the traveller from Ambleside to the dramatic Wrynose and Hardknott Passes and over to the western side of the Lake District. Get away from the road and you will find it is indeed one of the many lovely corners to be explored on foot. Near the head of the valley and before you climb to Wrynose Pass, turn right and to the north and you will climb on to the hause (a narrow neck of land) between Little Langdale and its more famous neighbour, Great Langdale. This area is rich in tarns, such as Little Langdale Tarn and Loughrigg Tarn, and is dominated by the Langdale Pikes themselves.

Little Langdale from Greenburn

The view from the old mine-workings at Greenburn is breathtaking. Looking east with Little Langdale Tarn below the view extends past Loughrigg Fell in the middle distance to the fells of Scandale and the Red Screes.

Little Langdale Tarn

Little Langdale Tarn is set in a bowl of land surrounded by an arc of fells. Seen here with Blake Rigg in the distance, this is always an oasis of peace. The natural lie of the land hides the narrow winding road that leads through the dale. You would be hard-pressed to pick out the road if it were not for the cottages at Fell Foot and Busk House. In fact the road enters at Wrynose Pass on the left, comes down into the valley bottom across the picture and then leaves on the right.

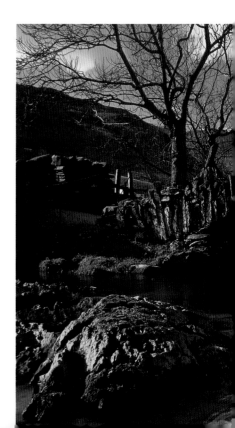

Greenburn Reservoir with Swirl How and Hell Gill Pike

Follow the route of Greenburn Beck up into the fells from Little Langdale Tarn and you will eventually come to Greenburn Reservoir. Originally built to support mine-workings, the small sheet of water sits beneath Weatherlam. In the distance the line of fells sweeps from Swirl How on the left round past Hell Gill Pike (2,172ft/662m) in the centre to the euphemistically named Wet Side Edge.

Slaters Bridge

Barely a few hundred yards downstream from the tarn is Slaters Bridge. Set in a glorious landscape with its lovely arch of local stone, this little bridge is a fine example of an old lakeland packhorse bridge. It must be one of the finest treasures of the Lake District; sadly, it has been necessary for safety reasons to instal a black metal handrail over its graceful form.

Great Langdale with Pike of Stickle

Known and loved by generations of fell-walkers, Great Langdale is a glacial valley which, from the evidence of the flood plain in this photograph, contained a sizeable lake in years gone by. Now the great fells tower above the green fields in which the Herdwick sheep, the traditional breed of the lakes, graze so peacefully. Bow Fell (2,959ft/902m), capped in snow, is seen on the left appearing over the flanks of the Langdale Pikes with Pike of Stickle (2,324/723m) showing on the right of the skyline.

Langdale Pikes

The fall of the light on the fells was never as important as in this photograph of the Langdale Pikes, taken near Blea Tarn. Every shadow plays its part in emphasising the graphic form and grandeur of the Pikes as they tower above the valleys hidden below.

Elterwater in late autumn light

Elterwater itself lies just down the valley from the village of the same name. This photograph is taken in late afternoon in mid November from High Close on the road that leads over from Grasmere. The autumn colours were at their very best and the low light streaming through the trees towards the camera lens captures the enchantment of autumn in the lakes.

Heather and stone with the Langdale Pikes

The heather on Lingmoor Fell acts as a colourful foreground and counterbalance to this view of the Langdale Pikes. In the distant shadows is the tumbling watercourse of Stickle Ghyll. The Pikes, a cluster of shapely hilltops, radiate out from Harrison Stickle at their centre. They provide some of the most dramatic ascents in the Lakes.

Blea Tarn and the Tilberthwaite Fells

This is one of the many views to be enjoyed from Lingmoor Fell, and includes Blea Tarn which is overlooked by Blake Rigg on the right. In the distance is the looming bulk of Weatherlam. The tarn and the valley bottom is bathed in beautiful late afternoon sunlight, which also picks out the heather in the foreground

Grasmere and Rydal Water

Loughrigg Fell separates Loughrigg Tarn and the popular and beautiful twin lakes of Grasmere and Rydal Water. These two lakes, which are steeped in the culture and history of the Lake District, have their own intimate qualities for the landscape photographer. While both are small enough to wander around in a single day, between them they have so many attractions that there is rarely enough time to explore them and the surrounding area.

Grasmere from Loughrigg Terrace

Grasmere is seen here from the slopes of Loughrigg Terrace, which has extensive views along the whole of its length. Looking northward to the village of Grasmere just beyond the lake, the gap in the skyline is Dunmail Raise, which the main road passes over on its way to Thirlmere. The gravel "beach" which you can see at the foot of the lake is a favourite with visitors for paddling and for picnics.

White Moss towards Easdale

The little fell of White Moss is situated between Grasmere and Rydal Water. Its top is a miniature wilderness of trees scattered among rocky hummocks with patches of marshland between. Here we look across the marshy land and its sunlit grasses with the two silver birches framing the distant snow-capped fell top of Sergeant Man (2,394ft/730m). On the left Silver How is in shadow.

Winter colours on Rydal

In the late afternoon the watery sun is just about to dip below the fells but is still strong enough to light up the little island and the trees on the left. The soft, muted colours of the background fells have already fallen into shadow.

Grasmere and the Lion and the Lamb

On a day of changing light with sun and shadows moving across the fells, this photograph of Grasmere shows the evocatively-named Lion and Lamb Fell in shadow, with the fells of Far Easdale catching the sunlight. The whole effect is enhanced by the band of sunshine which gives a lift to the area around the lake and highlights the homesteads along the shore.

Rydal Water southside

At the close of the year, with all the summer walkers and picnickers gone, the lakeside walk around Rydal Water takes on a wonderfully peaceful mood. For those who venture out there is the reward of the dramatic winter colours, which are so evident in this photograph of one of the Lake District's most popular beauty spots.

The central valleys

The central valleys of the Lake District are located on either side of Grasmere and Rydal Water – and form the main north-south route through the Lakes. To the north is Thirlmere and the watershed of Dunmail Raise and to the south, Ambleside and Windermere. Kirkstone Pass, at 1,489ft (454m) is the highest road pass in the Lake District and guards the southern approach to the region. This is an area of high, desolate moorland with many fast-flowing streams and waterfalls. The long, thin lake of Thirlmere, which lies to the north, is one of the few lakes accessible by car or on foot.

Stock Ghyll waterfall

Stock Ghyll Force, a dramatic waterfall on a tributary of the River Rothay, is a short walk from the centre of Ambleside. In the past, Stock Ghyll powered a number of watermills to fuel local industry. Photographically, waterfalls can often look at their best on a dull day. Using a slow shutter speed, coupled with a tripod, the waters of Stock Ghyll jump out from their cluttered surroundings, and there is a real sensation of movement as water crashes down the falls.

St John's in the Vale with Blencathra

St John's in the Vale may have no lake to boast of but it does have an enthusiastic band of followers who love its rugged scenery. You only have to walk a short distance on to the fells, as seen here under the lea of Helvellyn, to experience glorious views. In the background Blencathra, with its familiar but dramatic skyline, sits astride the northern end of the vale with Rake Howe looming in the middle distance.

Cold winter tree

In this photograph of the fellside in St John's in the Vale you can almost feel the cold of winter. St John's links Blencathra, one of the Lake District's most dramatic peaks, and Thirlmere via an impressively steep valley. This evocatively named area contains many remnants of the old quarrying industry.

Brothers Water to Haweswater

Continue over the Kirkstone Pass and down the other side and you will soon come to the little glacial lake of Brothers Water as it nestles into Patterdale. This is another of those small peaceful locations where the lake can, occasionally, remain tranquil for much of the day. You can either take a gentle stroll around the lake, or be more energetic and climb up into the surrounding fells. Alternatively, you could walk from the little village of Hartsop near the foot of the lake, up onto the Knott and Angle Crags, to view the mountain tarns and reservoirs. Or, if you continue over the fell via the route of the Coast to Coast walk, you will experience the dramatic surroundings of the Haweswater reservoir.

Winter light on the reeds

One can never fail to be attracted to the splendid bank of reeds that surrounds the head of Brothers Water, especially when the light shines on them. The light was exceptionally good on the New Year's Eve when this photograph was taken, providing a contrast between the almost luminous, sunlit rushes and the more subdued bluish-white of the snow-clad fell behind. A lonely waterfowl ploughs its solitary way through the icy water.

View across to Hartsop

As you walk along the track that skirts the western side of Brothers Water your view of the lake is constantly interrupted by the trees that grow down to the water's edge. This photograph is taken across the lake towards the village of Hartsop with Brock Crags towering behind. It almost conveys the feeling that you are peering through the trees to the village in the distance.

Sheep reflections

This tranquil scene of sheep on the shoreline at Brothers Water was almost taken by chance. The sheep were suddenly spotted at the water's edge, beautifully grouped at the edge of the lake. The clear reflections, even at midday, coupled with the effect of the backlighting on the reeds, helped to create this picture.

Brothers Water from the outflow

Brothers Water, a quiet glacial lake, lies in Patterdale at the foot of Kirkstone Pass. This little lake is sheltered from the wind and its peaceful location gives rise to superb reflections that can remain all day. This photograph was taken on an early spring morning. The combination of a shimmering reflection combined with the light and shadow caused by the clouds passing overhead accentuates the beauty of this lake which is surrounded by the high fells.

View towards Dovedale

A September walk along the eastern shore of Brothers Water brings this colourful shot across the lake towards Dovedale. There is just a hint of the forthcoming autumn colour which is enhanced by the water lily leaves to the bottom right. The little white puffy cloud in an otherwise clear blue sky adds an interesting touch.

27

Hayswater and High Street from Satura Crag

Carry on past Angle Tarn and you will shortly find yourself on Satura Crag, a rocky outcrop which overlooks Hayswater. This little pool of water, among the rocks on Satura Crag, is only a few feet across but makes a fine foreground to this photograph. This panoramic scene, with its spectacular sky, shows Hayswater with High Street Fell in the distance. High Street is part of the route of an old Roman road and horse races used to be held each year on its summit.

Mardale in changeable weather

Further up Haweswater is Mardale. This village was submerged when the Haweswater valley was flooded in 1935 to provide water for the city of Manchester. In this photograph you can clearly see the scarred waterline of the reservoir.

Riggindale and the reservoir

Water levels can significantly change the appearance of a reservoir such as Haweswater. This photograph was taken on a day of changeable weather in autumn when the water level was low after a period of dry weather. The islands have enlarged and merged into one and, on the far side, where Riggindale meets the reservoir, field patterns from the past, normally submerged, have been exposed to view.

Haweswater and the far fells

This is a panoramic view across Haweswater on a fine February day. The impressive line of snow-covered hills at the far side shows Illgill (1,998ft/609m) on the left, Eagle Crag (1,709ft/521m) in the centre and High Street (2,717ft/828m) at the back and to the right.

Winter view toward Kidsty Howe

In this view of Haweswater, Riggindale can be seen in the far distance to the left, with Kidsty Howe to its right, where Wainwright's Coast to Coast walk starts its descent out of the Lakeland fells. There are no true reflections on this day but there is still a sheen on the otherwise blue water caused by the light from the snow-clad fells catching on the surface of the reservoir.

Ullswater

The final part of our journey takes us down Patterdale from Brothers Water to Ullswater, the second largest lake in the Lake District. In the summer, the lake is dotted with the colourful sails of yachts and steamers cruise its length. Yet it is one of those places that always feels intimate despite its size. From Pooley Bridge, the lake stretches in a south-westerly direction for about eight miles. Around almost every corner are little gems to be explored and enjoyed. It is a place to linger and return to often; in spring and summer, when the sunrises can be spectacular, and into the autumn, when the colours of the beeches along the lakesides are second to none, to winter when the light is at its very best.

Place Fell from Glenridding

In the sheltered area of water near the head of Ullswater, at Glenridding, the reflections can remain well into the day. This photograph was taken at approximately 11am when all the conditions seemed right. Late November snows dust Place Fell, so that the autumn colours are mixed with a touch of winter. The still waters of Ullswater with their almost perfect reflection complete the scene.

Ullswater sunrise

In summer the sunrises over Ullswater can be spectacular. This photograph was taken just after 5.30am in August, when the sun was rising in a clear eastern sky and the light was bouncing off the cloud cover over the lake. The result was this dramatic and colourful scene – just one of a number of varied shots taken during a glorious hour or so that day.

Ullswater morning – the boathouse

As you approach Ullswater from the direction of the main A66 this is the very first view that you get of a lake in the Lake District. If you can catch it in conditions such as these it is without doubt one of the most stunning views that you will see in the whole of this area of outstanding natural beauty. This photograph was taken shortly after sunrise with the mist clearing from the lake and the sun lighting up the old boathouse. Five minutes later the mists had cleared and the reflection was lost, but the magic of those few minutes will remain forever.

Tree framing golden bracken

It is not only trees which provide autumn colour – the golden-coloured bracken below the trees can also add to the glory that is autumn in Ullswater. In this photograph, framed by a craggy old oak tree, we look through to the glorious golden colours beyond. In Glencoyne Wood there is a network of paths which allow you to enjoy these autumnal scenes yet still have excellent views over Ullswater.

Gowbarrow dawn light

This view looks across Ullswater in the light of dawn near Gowbarrow – the spot which inspired the Lake District's most famous son, the Romantic poet William Wordsworth, to write his best-loved poem on the subject of daffodils. The photograph catches the reflected light of a winter sunrise and, with its rose-tinted hues, brilliantly reflects the glory of dawn in the lakes.

First published in 2009 by Myriad Books Limited
35 Bishopsthorpe Road, London SE26 4PA

Photographs and text copyright © Dave Coates

Dave Coates has asserted his right under the Copyright, Designs and
Patents Act, 1988, to be identified as the author of this work

ISBN 1 84746 242 1
EAN 978 1 84746 242 8

Designed by Jerry Goldie

Printed in China